Drawn from Life

Three Generations of Wyeth Figure Studies

By Victoria Browning Wyeth

Cooperstown, New York
FenimoreArt.org

Victoria Browning Wyeth, Guest Curator
Christine Rossi, Co-Curator, Director of Exhibitions

Published by Fenimore Art Museum
5798 State Highway 80
Cooperstown, New York 13326 USA
FenimoreArt.org

Managing Editors
Victoria Browning Wyeth
Christine Rossi

Catalogue Design
Melodee Dill Stephens
Brilliant Graphics
Exton, PA

Printed in the U.S.A.
Brilliant Graphics
Exton, PA

Published in Conjunction with the Exhibition
Drawn from Life: Three Generations of Wyeth Figure Studies, on view at
Fenimore Art Museum, Cooperstown, NY, May 7–September 5, 2022

Exhibition Curators
Victoria Browning Wyeth, Guest Curator
Christine Rossi, Director of Exhibitions

Exhibition Management and Design
Christine Rossi, James Matson, Martha Membrino, Christine Olsen, Tina Yagjian

Exhibition Sponsors
The Clark Foundation
C. J. Heilig Foundation
The Tom Morgan and Erna J. McReynolds Charitable Foundation
NYCM Insurance
Mr. and Mrs. Thomas O. Putnam
This project is supported by a Market New York grant awarded to Fenimore Art Museum from I LOVE NY/
New York State's Division of Tourism through the Regional Economic Development Council initiative.

ISBN 978-0-917334-53-5

Table of Contents

cover

Untitled (#2313), 1936
Andrew Wyeth | Charcoal on paper
Collection of the Wyeth Foundation for American Art

Foreword

This exhibition and catalogue mark the third important collaboration with Victoria Wyeth, granddaughter of Andrew Wyeth, and her extended family. *Drawn from Life: Three Generations of Wyeth Figure Studies* builds upon our previous projects, *Andrew Wyeth at 100: A Family Remembrance* (2017) and *The Wyeths: A Family Legacy* (2013). All three share the unique perspective of one of America's most important artistic families looking at itself. *Drawn from Life* focuses upon how the Wyeths became such masters of human anatomy through persistence, dedication, and hard work.

This has been a family endeavor in every sense. We are grateful to our friend and colleague Victoria Wyeth for once again expertly curating an in-depth exploration of her family's sublime artistry. We are also grateful for the contributions of Victoria's father, Nicky Wyeth, and her uncle, Jamie Wyeth, both of whom offered their insights into the artwork. Victoria's aunt, Judy Kopff, assisted with editing.

We owe a debt of gratitude to the lenders to this exhibition, without whom it would have been impossible to effectively tell the story of the artmaking of the Wyeths. They include: Brandywine River Museum of Art (Thomas Padon, The James H. Duff Director, and Sarah Buehler, Registrar); The Phyllis and Jamie Wyeth Collection (Jamie Wyeth and Mary Beth Dolan); The Wyeth Foundation for American Art, Andrew Wyeth Offices (Mary Landa, Karen Baumgartner, and Amy Morey); LaSalle University Art Museum; Colquitt County Arts Center; Portland Museum of Art; and private collectors Debra Campbell, Dan Ostermiller, and Thomas Carpenter Keiper.

Our funders, of course, also played a large role in making this project possible. We are grateful to The Clark Foundation, the C. J. Heilig Foundation, The Tom Morgan and Erna J. Morgan McReynolds Charitable Foundation, NYCM Insurance, and Mr. and Mrs. Thomas O. Putnam. This project is also supported by a Market New York grant awarded to Fenimore Art Museum from I LOVE NY/New York State's Division of Tourism through the Regional Economic Development Council initiative.

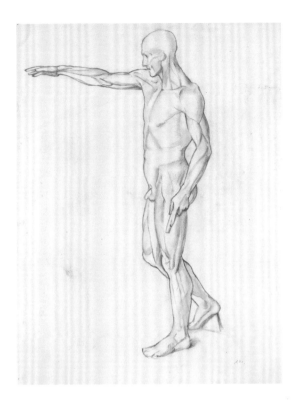

Untitled (#2272r), 1935
Andrew Wyeth | Pencil on paper
Collection of the Wyeth Foundation
for American Art

Andy, like his father, N.C., drew from plaster casts of the figure to better understand the body. An artist's study of anatomy was usually limited to figure drawing classes, anatomy books, and the use of plaster casts. Jamie, who also drew this cast, later took the study of anatomy a step further with his dissections and then drawings of human cadavers, also seen in this exhibition.

Our exceptional staff make these projects happen through hard work, creativity, and steadfast dedication. For this project, I extend a special thanks to Director of Exhibitions Christine Rossi, who worked closely with Victoria and the Wyeth family throughout the process, as she did with the previous exhibitions.

This exhibition and catalogue are, above all, a tribute to the commitment and passion of the artists: N.C. Wyeth, Carolyn Wyeth, Andrew Wyeth, and Jamie Wyeth. Together they have created an artistic legacy that continues to resonate with people of all backgrounds who find profound meaning in an art that is true to the life from which it is drawn.

Paul S. D'Ambrosio, Ph.D.
President & CEO
Fenimore Art Museum

Drawn from Life

Three Generations of Wyeth Figure Studies

Introduction

The figure lies at the heart of much of my family's work, and the foundations were laid in the early classroom and studio studies they created in their adolescence and early 20s. N.C. Wyeth's early sketches show the promise of his later illustrations, while Andy's show his father's guidance in explaining the figure. Jamie's anatomical work provides a deeper dive into understanding the figure at its most elemental level.

Looking at the early anatomical drawings by my family gives us a peek into the beginnings of their careers as artists, acute observers of their environment, and brilliant draftsmen. Without these basic figurative drawings, we never would have had Blind Pew from N.C.'s *Treasure Island*, Christina Olson from Andy's *Christina's World*, or Jamie's countless paintings of Rudolf Nureyev. In examining these early works, we gain insight into the artistic process encountered by all three generations. To paraphrase my Uncle Jamie, studies, like these many, never-before displayed early works, represent "a doorway" to the work that was to come.

My thanks to my Uncle Jamie for his help and support. His voice, along with quotes from my grandfather, Andy, and insights from my father, Nicky, inform and bring to life this exhibition.

Victoria Browning Wyeth

Untitled (seated male nude), ca. 1900
N.C. Wyeth | Charcoal on paper
Collection of Colquitt County Arts Center, Frank McCall Jr. Permanent Collection
SUPP2000.1475

The gesture and pose of this model are similar in feeling to Andy's study for *Undercover*. Andy's son Nicky relates them to the nineteenth-century American artist Thomas Eakins: *"[Eakins] was using live [nude] models even though he was chastised for it. I don't think there is any question, early on, that N.C. was influenced by him."* This influence can be seen in other works by Andy and Jamie in this exhibition.

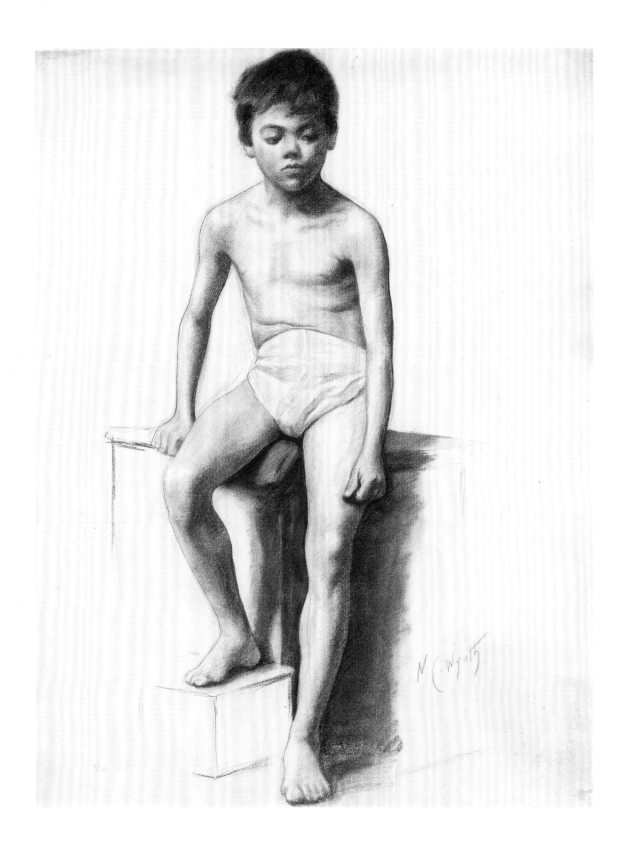

I.
Academic Studies

My great-grandfather, N.C. Wyeth, ALWAYS stressed the importance of academic studies for all his children. Instructed by N.C. in his studio, Carolyn and Andy endlessly drew cubes, bottles, and plaster figure casts before progressing to nude models. Although N.C.'s training with artist Howard Pyle was quite different—Pyle, an illustrator, stressed the importance of costumes and props for models—both men understood the value of fine training when beginning a career as an artist. During his conversations with author James Duff in 1986, Andy remembered his father as *"a great teacher. When it came to cast drawings, his other students never did any. But we kids were something different. We did them."*

 Carolyn not only understood but echoed the importance of studying cones, spheres, and plaster busts when teaching my Uncle Jamie. Clearly, she employed the same methods her father had used but added a touch of humor and eccentricity. Carolyn was larger than life and infused her personality into her teaching. She was a wonderful and encouraging teacher, and she made it fun for my uncle. He explained, *"I loved being in the studio because she dressed like him. She wore his clothes—his knickers and his black hat, for example. It was fascinating to me because I spent my childhood looking at his illustrations, which were all stacked up there, and then to have him embodied in her was sort of 'whoa.'"*

Study of a Young Male Model, ca. 1900
N.C. Wyeth | Charcoal on paper
Private collection, Wilmington, Delaware

N.C. Wyeth expressed his love of art early, studying watercolor by the age of 12 under the tutelage of Cora Livingstone, a Needham, Massachusetts, neighbor. The early figure studies shown in this exhibition are most likely from N.C. Wyeth's time at the Eric Pape School of Art in Boston, where he studied illustration. While his mother supported his attendance at art school, N.C.'s father cautioned, *"You can't make a living as an artist!"*

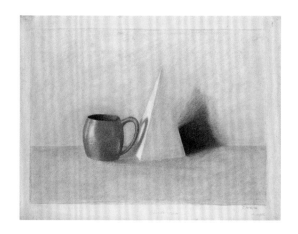

Ludwig van Beethoven, ca. 1925
Carolyn Wyeth | Pencil on paper
Brandywine River Museum of Art
Purchased with Museum funds, 2010

Carolyn and her brother Andy studied exclusively
with their father, N.C., in his studio behind the house
in Chadds Ford, Pennsylvania. Their sister, Henriette,
also an artist, studied with N.C. and later at the
Pennsylvania Academy of Fine Arts. As part of their
training, the Wyeth children were compelled to draw
from plaster models.

Carolyn, whose work outside the classroom was
free and imaginative, found the drawing exercises
annoying. Jamie observed that Carolyn's sketch of the
mask of Beethoven. *". . . is just beautifully done. . . .
But it bears no relation to her other work. It is like
a different hand."* When Jamie asked his Aunt
Henriette about that, she said, *"Pa just imposed on
Carolyn, 'You WILL draw this as it is.' And she did
finally . . . I think she handled charcoal better than
almost anyone I know."*

Still Life with Pyramid and Mug, ca. 1932
Carolyn Wyeth | Charcoal on paper
Brandywine River Museum of Art
Gift of Mr. and Mrs. Andrew Wyeth, 1985

Carolyn taught her students, including her nephew
Jamie, using the same techniques as her father, N.C.
Jamie remembered, *"She got me to do cubes and
spheres, which I hate. . . . They're just basic shapes. Part
of the training. Get used to shapes. In other words, no
artifices, no color. It is just the black and white sphere
and the shadow it creates."*

Carolyn also influenced Jamie's choice of medium,
oil paint. Jamie explained, *"As a child, I would go
into her studio. She had a little studio attached to the
N.C. Wyeth studio. And she would have me prepare
her palette. I would squirt the paint; I loved the
consistency of it."*

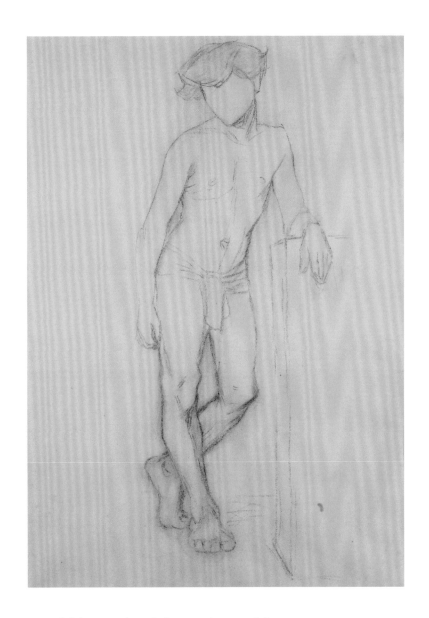

Untitled (semi-nude male figure with proper left
hand resting on waist-high box), ca. 1900
N.C. Wyeth | Charcoal or pencil on paper
Collection of Mr. Dan Ostermiller
Photograph by Richard Walker

In this early work, Jamie saw N.C.'s development of gesture and use of line:
"Almost like a Cezanne drawing . . . the way the figure is done. The way he suggested
the head but decided 'to hell with the face' and just did the gesture of the figure is
taking it further than just drawing exactly what he saw. He is making choices."

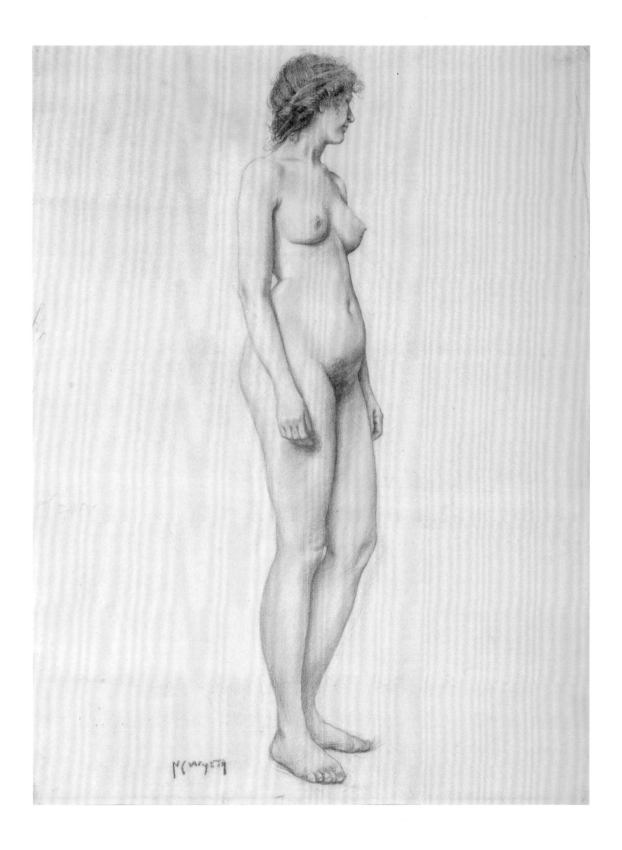

Untitled (standing female nude), 1900–1901
N.C. Wyeth | Charcoal or pencil on paper
Collection of LaSalle University Art Museum
SUPP2000.1528 | 75-D-63

This work displays N.C.'s growing understanding of the figure and his potential to imbue them with life, something for which he would later become known. Jamie explained, *"You really feel it's a human being standing there. And to do that just in black and white. I'm astounded that he was so young when he did this work."*

Untitled (#2280), 1935
Andrew Wyeth | Pencil on paper
Collection of the Wyeth Foundation for American Art

In this sketch of a typical figure pose, we see Andy figuring out the curve of the model's spine with the help of his father. Faintly sketched to the right you can see N.C. demonstrating the curve and angle of the back, all key to making a figure come to life, something at which he excelled. Andy's son Nicky recalled his grandfather's mastery of the figure: *"In my grandfather's work, you can feel the impact—muscles are ready to jump out at you."*

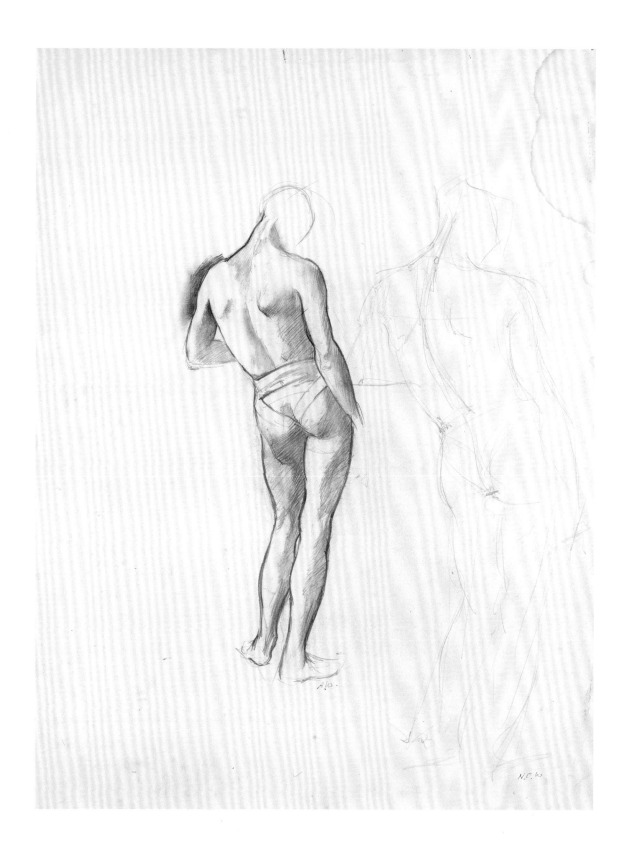

II.

Figure Studies

When Andy, my grandfather, first began painting around the age of 10, his work was filled with imagination: war drawings of soldiers being blown apart in battle or charging toward each other, knights fighting in the forest, pirates on the beach, or Paul Revere in the moonlight. He would line up his toy soldiers and create an imaginary world fueled by his own stories. Before his academic training began, his father, N.C., showed his son how to get more "life in his pictures" by having Andy draw a scene (such as Native Americans in the woods) and then recreating the scene below Andy's drawing.

This process all changed when he entered his father's studio at the age of 15 on October 19, 1932. In a 1959 *Cosmopolitan* magazine article, Andy noted: *"My father was not concerned with formal [school] training. He often said that no good painter went to college. But he wanted me to see clearly. He taught me anatomy, made me draw from casts, brought in nude models—did everything in his power to help me see."* Not only did Andy learn to see, he also mastered the figure. He drew the human body from every possible angle: back, front, left standing, left sitting, and more. It's interesting to note that my grandfather put the models in their positions, not N.C.

Untitled (#2315), 1936
Andrew Wyeth | Charcoal on paper
Collection of the Wyeth Foundation for American Art

Jamie saw this work as more than a simple classroom study: *"I think it is such an interesting characterization of somebody. It goes beyond an anatomy study or a figure study . . . the composition is fascinating."*

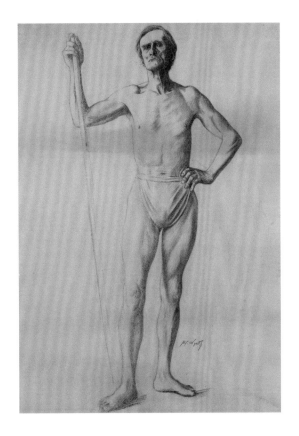

Untitled (Male figure standing with pole), 1900
N.C. Wyeth | Charcoal or pencil on paper
Collection of Mr. Dan Ostermiller
Photograph by Richard Walker

Untitled (#2328), 1936
Andrew Wyeth | Charcoal on paper
Collection of the Wyeth Foundation for American Art

The models in these two studies take on standing poses commonly used in figure
drawing classes. N.C. would have repeated these exercises for Andy's figure-drawing
sessions. Although he was studying with N.C., Andy could pose the models as
he liked. In his study, Andy has the model's back turned to the viewer—a more
intriguing pose and one that Andy would use in later work.

Untitled (Model dressed as a Puritan), 1901–1902
N.C. Wyeth | Charcoal on paper
Collection of the Wyeth Foundation for American Art
SUPP2000.969

N.C. Wyeth's early figure sketches, such as this one, are capable renderings of the figure. Training in his home state of Massachusetts prepared him to understand and realistically depict the figure, which set the stage for his illustrative work.

Untitled (Study of woman in kimono), ca. 1902
N.C. Wyeth | Charcoal on laid paper
Portland Museum of Art, Maine, Museum purchase, 1982.180
Image courtesy of Luc Demers

In this study of a costumed woman, N.C. captures the model's pensive pose through the tilt of her head and direction of her gaze. The study is incomplete, with the fan and robe simply described in line, an aspect that Jamie often finds more interesting than a fully rendered subject: *"I like things incomplete."*

Untitled (Study, bust of an African American man), 1900–1901
N.C. Wyeth | Charcoal on laid paper
Collection of the Wyeth Foundation for American Art
SUPP2000.2266

N.C.'s early classroom portraits explore the face and the sitter's character. Andy spoke about a more serene quality contained in some of his father's later portraiture. In an interview with author James Duff, Andy recalled N.C. explaining, *"When my mother died, I took the train right to Needham. . . . I went up and sat there with her . . . studying that face lying there on that white pillow. . . . It made such an impression on me. It changed everything for me."*

After N.C and his grandson Newell were killed in a car accident in 1945, Andy returned to Chadds Ford and sat with their bodies before the funeral. He experienced a similar revelatory experience: *"I remembered what my father said. He was so right. Their faces had become masks of eternity."*

Untitled (#2297), 1938
Andrew Wyeth | Pencil on paper
Collection of the Wyeth Foundation for American Art

My grandfather, like many artists, began doing self-portraits as a young man. Early on, they were rather formal (for example, sitting in front of his easel, walking through the fields of Chadds Ford, and staring at a mirror). This all changed in 1949, however, when he began to infuse his imagination into his art as seen in *The Revenant*. The painting depicts Andy's ghostly reflection in a dusty mirror at the home of his friends, Christina and Alvaro Olson, in Maine.

Untitled (#2290), 1936
Andrew Wyeth | Charcoal on paper
Collection of the Wyeth Foundation for American Art

Chadds Ford neighbor Martin Leonard was the subject for this
study. Andy frequently asked local friends and neighbors to pose,
a practice that Jamie has continued.

Untitled (#2313), 1936
Andrew Wyeth | Charcoal on paper
Collection of the Wyeth Foundation
for American Art

Untitled (#2320), 1936
Andrew Wyeth | Charcoal on paper
Collection of the Wyeth Foundation
for American Art

Young artists try out styles and techniques, influenced by other
artists and their teachers. To Jamie, these two works by his father
appeared loose and more expressive than Andy's other early
sketches. With their strong lines, Jamie described them as
". . . really impressionistic. Very painterly, almost like brush strokes."

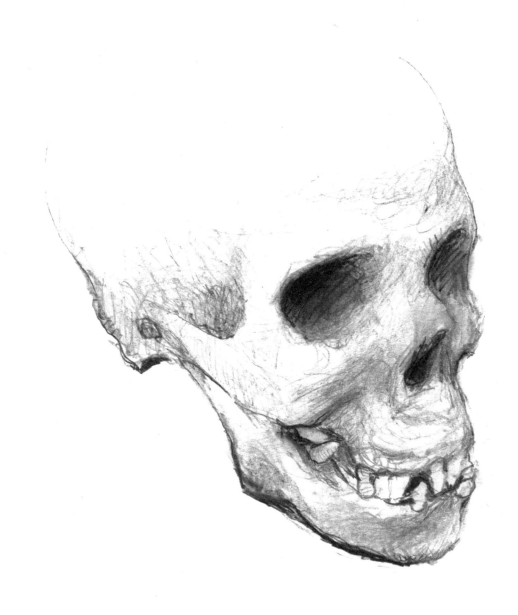

III.

Anatomy

The first female nude that my grandfather painted was a plaster model. I remember him telling me, *"I was so excited to finally paint a female nude, and then Pa pulled out this statue."* When Andy graduated to live models, N.C. had local friends and neighbors come and pose for him so that he could meticulously obsess over every muscle and fold and crease in the body. In his early anatomy drawings, we see a young artist exploring the body. He's looking at details—hands, feet, and the folds of the ears. Although many of these drawings lack the emotion of his later figurative work, this was the beginning of his understanding of the figure.

My Uncle Jamie has an unparalleled love of the macabre, so it should come as no surprise that to understand anatomy fully, he went to the place where he could find an endless supply of individuals who would never complain that they were tired or that their necks hurt from holding a pose: the morgue. As a young artist, my uncle was acutely aware of the fact that studying dissection would provide a deep (and much needed) understanding of how the human body worked. It helped him to understand the underlying structures and how they informed what the external features looked like. When asked why he chose the morgue, he noted, *"I just was curious why there was a crease here in somebody's face. I mean, you actually dissect it. You see what it was. And I don't think you ever forget."* Quite simply, he wanted to know *"why that bump was there."*

Morgue Drawing Skull, 1965
Jamie Wyeth | Pencil on paper, anatomical sketchbook, page 8
The Phyllis and Jamie Wyeth Collection

Art students sometimes observe dissections at a medical school where the focus is more on internal systems and less on what animates a figure. Jamie's dissections and studies allowed him to focus on how the body moved and looked. Through his studies, Jamie was able to internalize the figure and bring that deep understanding to his work.

Untitled (#2270), 1935

Andrew Wyeth | Pencil on paper

Collection of the Wyeth Foundation for American Art

As with a reclining figure, rendering a full-length torso and its proportions is challenging. As Andy works out the overall form, he is also exploring the details of the ears and the gesture of the hands.

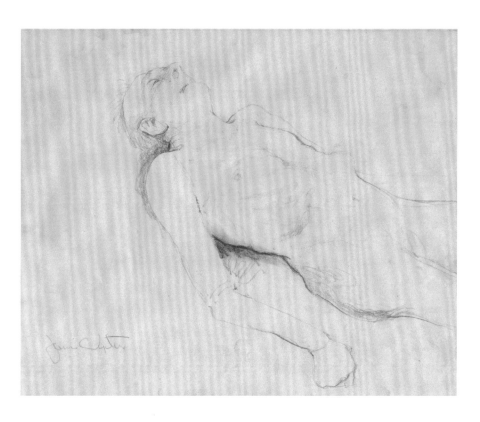

Morgue Drawing, Cadaver, 1965
Jamie Wyeth | Pencil on paper
Collection of the Wyeth Foundation
for American Art

Untitled (#2310), 1935
Andrew Wyeth | Pencil on paper
Collection of the Wyeth Foundation
for American Art

Each of these studies, one by Jamie and the other
by Andy, uses foreshortening to depict the body
realistically from a difficult angle. The proportions
are intentionally altered to put the figure in
perspective, a technique that requires practice
and an understanding of the figure. The object of
these studies, as with the others shown here, is to
understand the figure so well that depicting it in
any pose comes naturally.

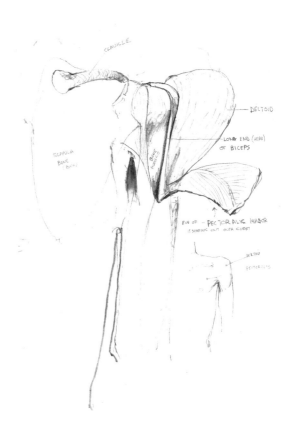

Morgue Drawing Deltoid, 1965
Jamie Wyeth | Pencil on paper,
anatomical sketchbook, page 1, recto
The Phyllis and Jamie Wyeth Collection

The anatomical dissection drawings in the exhibition
come from the sketchbook that Jamie used in the
morgue. The idea of studying gross anatomy was first
sparked by Jamie's love of Thomas Eakins' anatomical
drawings. Jamie connected with a Russian anatomist
at the Vagelos College for Physicians and Surgeons at
Columbia University who had seen Jamie's work in an
exhibition in the former Soviet Union. The anatomist
was doing a study of the comparative anatomy of
limbs and their articulation, and his lab contained
dismembered arms and legs, which intrigued Jamie.

Over time, Jamie became fascinated, electrified,
and obsessed with better understanding the human
form. This obsession with his subject matter is a
thread that continues to weave itself through every
piece of art that my uncle creates.

Morgue Drawing Clavicle, 1965
Jamie Wyeth | Pencil on paper,
anatomical sketchbook, page 6
The Phyllis and Jamie Wyeth Collection

Morgue Drawing Neck, 1965
Jamie Wyeth | Pencil on paper, anatomical
sketchbook, page 7
The Phyllis and Jamie Wyeth Collection

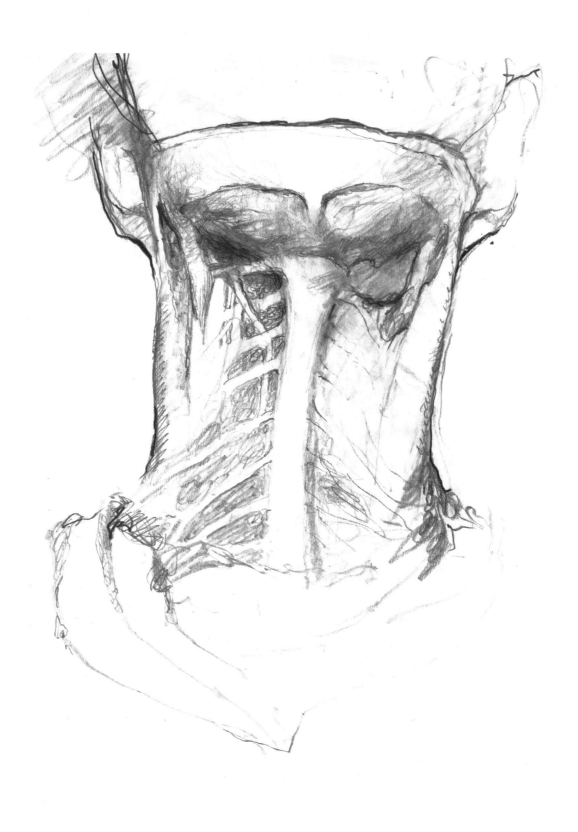

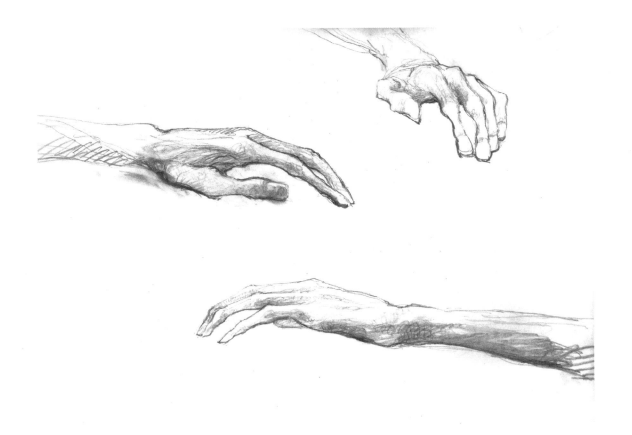

Morgue Drawing Three Hands, 1965
Jamie Wyeth | Pencil on paper, anatomical sketchbook, page 5
The Phyllis and Jamie Wyeth Collection

Jamie noted, *". . . hands are very difficult, I think because they are so expressive.
Portrait painters always have a terrible time with the hands."* Understanding
how the muscles, tendons, and bones work is key to depicting them naturally.
*"I was working on [a cadaver's] arm and hand, so I clamped the tendons and
made the hand finally pick up my pencil."*

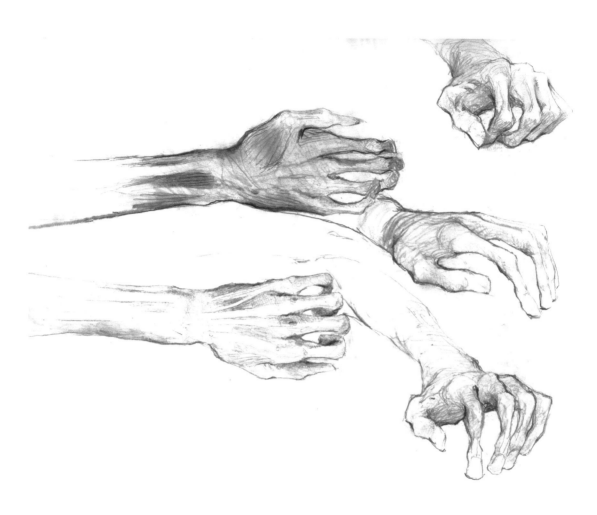

Morgue Drawing Five Hands, 1965
Jamie Wyeth | Pencil on paper, anatomical sketchbook, page 4
The Phyllis and Jamie Wyeth Collection

Untitled (#2276), 1935
Andrew Wyeth | Pencil on paper
Collection of the Wyeth Foundation for American Art

Andy's understanding of hands was gained through numerous sessions in the studio, while Jamie's understanding is informed by his anatomical studies. Both Jamie's and Andy's figurative work is influenced by N.C. My father, Nicky, remarked, *"Andy's rendering of hands is very much like my grandfather's. The bigness of them. My grandfather was a master at doing hands. If you look at his illustrations, the hands are incredible."*

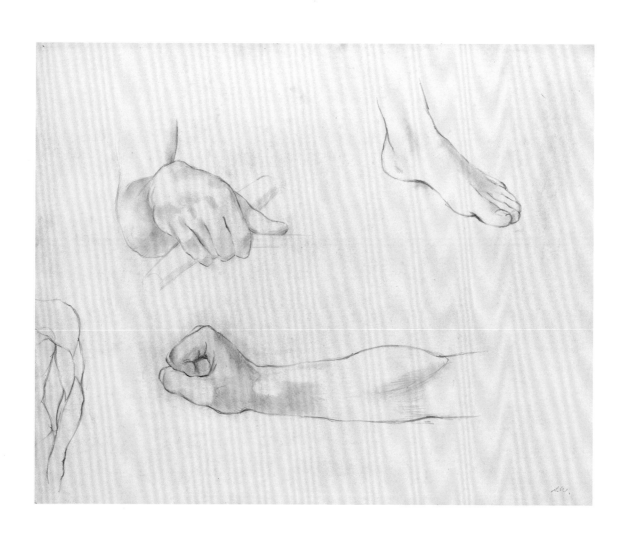

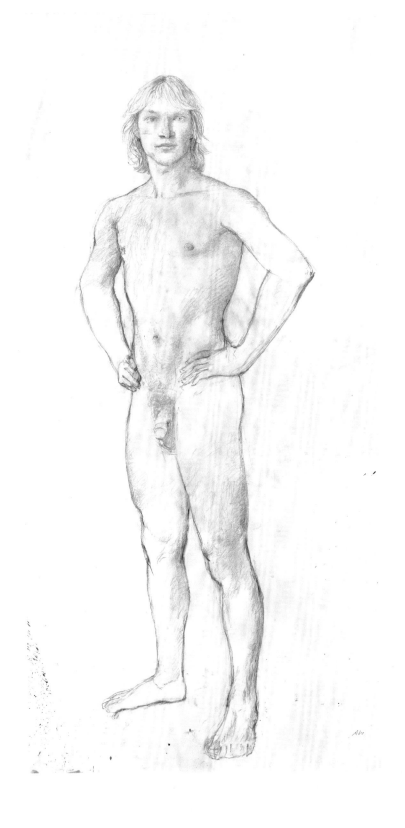

IV.
The Model

Painting models, whether they were friends, family, strangers, or animals (dead or alive), was a massive part of life for Andy, as it is for my Uncle Jamie. Sometimes the model was someone my grandfather had known since the model was a small child (such as our family friend, Johnny Lynch), while other times they were people who came and went.

When I asked my grandfather how he met the people who posed for him, he explained, *"I naturally come across models."* In other words, Andy painted the people he knew, the people he loved, and the people who were a part of his life. The better he knew his model, the more comfortable he was painting that person. He often moved around his model, sometimes coming within two or three inches of the person's face to study the eyelashes or the corner of the mouth. He wanted nothing more than to take a close look. He said, *"I think that's what makes my art different from that of a lot of other painters. You can look at it from a distance, but if you look up close, you'll see more dimension. I put a lot of detail into it."*

Although Andy never taught Jamie formally, my grandfather did offer numerous lessons. First and foremost: paint what you know and paint what you love. Much like his father, Jamie said, *"The things that I have painted are the things that I have seen all my life. Nothing interests me less than an interesting face. . . . What does interest me, and I don't know what triggers it, is something that the person exudes . . . and then I feel, 'Oh, my God, I've got to record this, this person.'"*

Image on page 38

The Clearing Study, 1979
Andrew Wyeth | Pencil on paper
Collection of the Wyeth Foundation
for American Art

Eric Standard was a young and handsome Finnish neighbor of ours in Maine. He was a close friend of my father, Nicky, and came for dinner on a regular basis. Andy often said he did not go looking for models, that he met them naturally, which was true in the case of both Eric and the Lynches.

It's interesting to understand the context in which the painting was done. Andy elaborated on the story when talking to author Tom Hoving: *"I finally had a hip operation and went up to Maine. I knew this handsome boy, Eric, an extraordinary specimen. There I was, hanging around with a crippled leg, and here was this perfect thing. The thought got me going—really to do him, totally nude. I was fascinated with that blonde hair coming down from his chest all the way to his pubic hair. The painting became more than a body; it was like finding a wonderful deer in the woods. It's sexually powerful—everything open, not sorted, just remarkable. . . . The point-counterpoint of him and myself—him so perfect and me with this crippled leg."*

Scuba Study, 1994
Andrew Wyeth | Pencil on paper
Collection of the Wyeth Foundation
for American Art

In the early 1990s, a young woman named Susan Miller began working for my grandparents as the caretaker for their islands (Allen and Benner) in Maine. Susan was a beautiful and tough New England woman. She posed only in the summer (because my grandparents came to Maine only from June to early October) and mostly posed on the island or at 8 Bells (N.C.'s studio).

This is an example of a composite portrait. Susan was unable to pose one day, and so my grandfather had a local friend, Dee Parker, step in as a model for Susan's body.

In the final painting, the pose is identical to the study. And while my grandfather was not one to put models in modern clothing, Susan, nonetheless, is depicted in a neoprene suit posing on the beach on Allen Island.

Undercover Study, 1970
Andrew Wyeth | Pencil on paper
Collection of the Wyeth Foundation for American Art

Johnny Lynch was my grandparents' neighbor in Chadds Ford, Pennsylvania. He and his brother, Jimmy, went to school with my Uncle Jamie and my father, Nicky, and Jimmy became one of my uncle's closest friends. It's interesting to note that both my grandfather and my uncle painted Jimmy Lynch over the years.

Andy describes his fascination with Johnny to author Tom Hoving: *"A real Lynch. I, frankly, was intrigued by his jet-black hair. Often my interest in a subject comes from an apparently insignificant detail. I liked his character. He was strong and quick."*

Undercover Study, 1970
Andrew Wyeth | Watercolor on paper
Collection of the Wyeth Foundation for American Art

Andy's initial drawings for his painting, *Undercover*, went through several transitions. At first, Johnny's back was to the viewer. As the drawings evolved, Johnny's position changed slightly. The final figure is evocative of those in Thomas Eakins' 1885 painting, the *Swimming Hole*.

As with N.C. and Jamie, Andy was inspired by Thomas Eakins' work and the artist's understanding of the human figure, gained through anatomical studies.

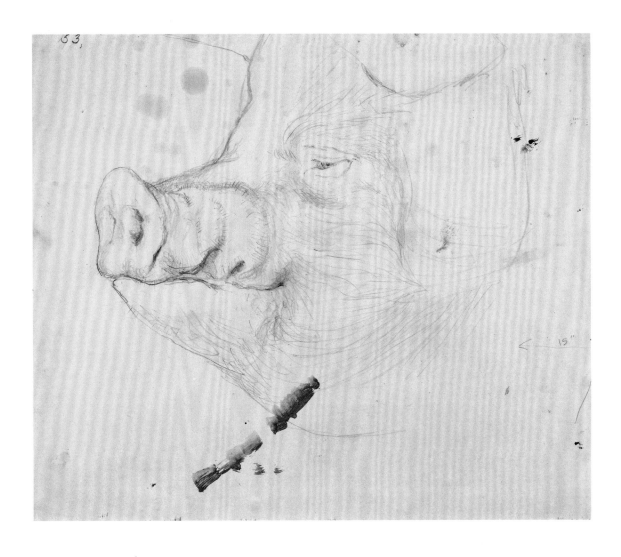

Pig Drawing, Head, 1969
Jamie Wyeth | Pencil on paper
All works from the Phyllis and Jamie Wyeth Collection

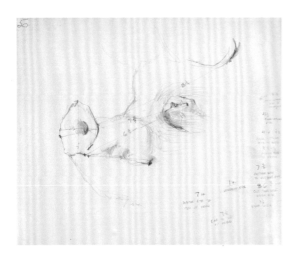

Pig Drawing, Head, 1969
Jamie Wyeth | Pencil on paper

Pig Drawing, Reclining, 1969
Jamie Wyeth | Pencil on paper

Jamie's Aunt Carolyn, also an animal lover, influenced his affinity for the pigs, sheep, chickens, and dogs that inhabit his paintings. Animals are depicted with the same level of care as humans. With both subjects, says Jamie, *"personality dictates the picture."*

When asked how he got his pig, Den Den, to sit still, Jamie noted, *"A pig farmer told me to play classical music. They do it on pig farms. They put music on, and it calms them down immediately. And she wanted to stand in the sunlight, so I wouldn't let her there unless she stood still."*

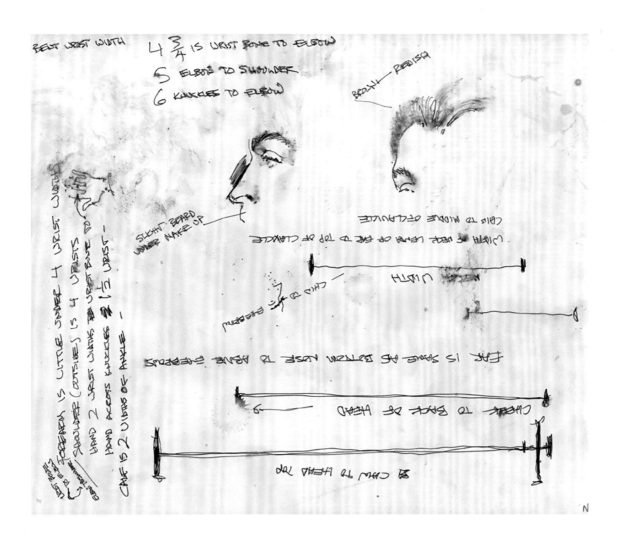

BELT WRIST WIDTH   4 3/4 IS WRIST BONE TO ELBOW
5 ELBOW TO SHOULDER
6 KNUCKLES TO ELBOW

BROWN - REDDISH

SLIGHT BEARD UNDER MAKE UP

CHIN TO MIDDLE OF CLAVICLE

WIDTH OF NECK LEVEL OF EAR TO TOP OF CLAVICLE

WIDTH

CHIN TO FOREARM

EAR IS SAME AS BOTTOM NOSE TO ABOVE EYEBROWS

CHEEK TO BACK OF HEAD

TO CHIN TO HEAD TOP

Sketchbook Image, N-31a, 1977

Jamie Wyeth | Pen and ink

Brandywine River Museum of Art, Purchased with funds from the Robert J. Kleberg, Jr. and Helen C. Kleberg Foundation; the Roemer Foundation; the Margaret Dorrance Strawbridge Foundation of PAI, Inc.; and an anonymous donor, 2006

Jamie uses calipers and other tools to measure the features of some of his models. When asked why he was so exacting for his portraits of Nureyev and Warhol, he responded, *"Because I just wanted to have it absolutely accurate. Nureyev kept saying, 'You measure so much you could make me [a] suit.' Warhol always called them the 'torture tools.'"*

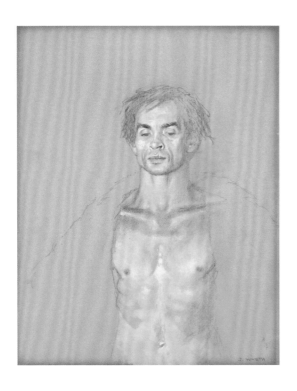

Unfinished Coat, in Fur, Nureyev (Study #13), 1977
Jamie Wyeth | Pencil and wash on paper
Brandywine River Museum of Art, Purchased with
funds given in memory of Dr. Margaret I. Handy, 1980

With some of his subjects (such as Nureyev, Warhol,
and John F. Kennedy), Jamie immersed himself in
their lives to such an extent that he could depict them
posthumously. Through his deep familiarity with them,
Jamie could *"bring them back to life, in a way. I did so
many studies of them that I could almost draw them in
any mood. Recreating their lives became fascinating."*

**Red Nureyev–The Phyllis M. Wyeth
"Nureyev Suite,"** 1977/2020
Jamie Wyeth | Charcoal, wash, gesso, and watercolor
on Twin Rocker Handmade Paper
The Phyllis and Jamie Wyeth Collection

My uncle moved to New York City in 1965 and started
work on a portrait of Lincoln Kirstein. A co-founder
of the New York City Ballet, Kirstein introduced
Jamie to the Russian ballet dancer Rudolf Nureyev,
and the two became great friends. Jamie's obsession
with the form that began in the morgue continued as
he carefully observed Nureyev dancing, resting, and
putting on makeup.

Defining the shape and gesture of the figure is essential
to rendering it. In this study my uncle outlined the
figure in black to "*. . . follow it and give the feeling of
his body.*" Jamie explained that from the time he first
started painting Nureyev, the dancer was comfortable
posing nude: "*The body was his tool. He wasn't
ashamed* [*to pose nude*]."

Jamie rediscovered this study after the death of his
wife, Phyllis Mills Wyeth, who was a great supporter
of the arts and a friend of Nureyev. The work is part
of a group of paintings that Phyllis had stashed away
starting in 1977.

Nureyev as the Faune, 1977 / 2002
Jamie Wyeth | Combined mediums on toned board
Brandywine River Museum of Art, Purchased with funds from the Robert J. Kleberg
Jr. and Helen C. Kleberg Foundation; Roemer Foundation; the Margaret Dorrance
Strawbridge Foundation of PAI, Inc; and an anonymous donor, 2006

There were countless times when my uncle observed and painted Nureyev in costume.
This painting is unusual because it demonstrates one of the few times that artist and model
collaborated. Nureyev was doing a production called *"Afternoon of a Faun."* He looked
at my uncle and said, *"Would you draw up something that may work as a costume?"*

About this painting, my uncle noted, *"This is a costume we worked out together.
If this all of a sudden jumped out at you, what would you do!?"*

Orca Bates (Study #1), 1990
Jamie Wyeth | Charcoal and conte crayon on brown cardboard
The Phyllis and Jamie Wyeth Collection

Orca Bates became the subject of many of Jamie's works *"because he just fascinated me as an individual. I was fascinated by his circumstances. At the age when I painted him, you didn't know if it was a boy or a girl. That fascinated me . . . and so I just wanted to make a record of it."*

The final portrait of Orca became *"like Jonah and the whale. You notice there is water on the floor by his feet. So, it's like he was part of the sea and came out from the inside of a whale. And there he appeared."* When asked about the inclusion of the digital watch, Jamie explained that he included it *"because it was contemporary at the time. I bounce between reality and imagination. And that is the whole point of painting."*

Wyeth Exhibition Checklist

Andy and Jamie on Monhegan Island, 1997
Victoria Browning Wyeth
Silver gelatin print
11″ x 14″
Collection of Fenimore Art Museum, Gift of Victoria Browning
Wyeth in memory of Andrew Wyeth
N0016.2018 (03)

N.C. WYETH (American, 1882–1945)

N.C. Wyeth
Adventure with a Giant Squid (Composition drawing), ca. 1940
Charcoal on paper
24 1/8″ x 15 1/2″
Brandywine River Museum of Art, Bequest of Carolyn Wyeth,
1996
96.1.544

N.C. Wyeth
Oisin in the Land of Youth (Composition drawing), 1940
Graphite on paper
29″ x 20 1/4″
Brandywine River Museum of Art, Bequest of Carolyn Wyeth,
1996
96.1.539

N.C. Wyeth
Untitled (Model dressed as a Puritan), 1901–1902
Charcoal on paper
28 1/4″ x 13″
Collection of the Wyeth Foundation for American Art
SUPP2000.969

N.C. Wyeth
Untitled (Study, bust of an African American man), 1900–1901
Charcoal on laid paper
24 3/8″ x 18 7/8″
Collection of the Wyeth Foundation for American Art
SUPP2000.2266

N.C. Wyeth
Untitled (Male model in velvet jacket, knickers, and ribboned
shoes, holding tri-cornered hat), 1900–1901
Probably charcoal on paper
28 3/8″ x 35 1/2″
Private Collection
(NCW1562)

N.C. Wyeth
Untitled (Semi-nude male figure with proper left hand
resting on waist-high box), ca. 1900
Charcoal or pencil on paper
28″ x 35″
Collection of Mr. Dan Ostermiller

N.C. Wyeth
Untitled (Nude male figure, standing, arms folded), 1900
Charcoal or pencil on paper
28″ x 35″
Collection of Mr. Dan Ostermiller

N.C. Wyeth
Untitled (Male figure standing with pole), 1900
Charcoal or pencil on paper
28″ x 35″
Collection of Mr. Dan Ostermiller

N.C. Wyeth
Untitled (Portrait), ca. 1900
Charcoal or pencil on paper
28″ x 35″
Collection of Mr. Dan Ostermiller

N.C. Wyeth
Untitled (Standing female nude), ca. 1900
Graphite on paper
24 1/2″ x 19″
Collection of LaSalle University Art Museum
SUPP2000.1528
75-D-63

N.C. Wyeth
Untitled (Seated male nude), ca. 1900
Charcoal on paper
23″ x 17″
Colquitt County Arts Center,
Frank McCall Jr. Permanent Collection
SUPP2000.1475

N.C. Wyeth (Newell Convers Wyeth, United States, 1882–1945)
Untitled (Study of woman in kimono), ca. 1902
Charcoal on laid paper
23 3/4″ x 18″
Portland Museum of Art, Maine, Museum purchase
1982.180

N.C. Wyeth
Study of a Young Male Model, ca. 1900
Charcoal on paper
24 3/4" x 18 1/2"
Private Collection, Wilmington, Delaware

CAROLYN WYETH (American, 1909–1994)

Carolyn Wyeth
Ludwig van Beethoven, ca. 1925
Pencil on paper
22 1/2" x 16 3/4"
Brandywine River Museum of Art,
Purchased with Museum funds, 2010

Carolyn Wyeth
Still Life with Pyramid and Mug, ca. 1932
19" x 25"
Charcoal on paper
Brandywine River Museum of Art,
Gift of Mr. and Mrs. Andrew Wyeth, 1985

Plaster Mask of Beethoven
P. P. Caproni & Brothers
18751925
Cast: plaster, iron, alloy, cotton
11" x 7 1/4" x 5"
Brandywine River Museum of Art, Bequest of Carolyn Wyeth, 1996

ANDREW WYETH (American, 1917–2009)

Andrew Wyeth
Untitled (#2322), 1935
Pencil on paper
19" x 25"
Collection of the Wyeth Foundation for American Art

Andrew Wyeth
Untitled (#2310), 1935
Pencil on paper
25" x 19"
Collection of the Wyeth Foundation for American Art

Andrew Wyeth
Untitled (#2276), 1935
Pencil on paper
19" x 24.88"
Collection of the Wyeth Foundation for American Art

Andrew Wyeth
Untitled (#2272r), 1935
Pencil on paper
25" x 19"
Collection of the Wyeth Foundation for American Art

Andrew Wyeth
Untitled (#2270), 1935
Pencil on paper
25" x 19"
Collection of the Wyeth Foundation for American Art

Andrew Wyeth
Untitled (#2280), 1935
Pencil on paper
25" x 19"
Collection of the Wyeth Foundation for American Art

Andrew Wyeth
Untitled (#2315), 1936
Charcoal on paper
24 1/2" x 18 3/4"
Collection of the Wyeth Foundation for American Art

Andrew Wyeth
Untitled (#2328), 1935
Pencil on paper
25" x 19"
Collection of the Wyeth Foundation for American Art

Andrew Wyeth
Untitled (#2313), 1936
Charcoal on paper
24 1/2" x 18 3/4"
Collection of the Wyeth Foundation for American Art

Andrew Wyeth
Untitled (#2290), 1936
Charcoal on paper
23.88" x 18.75"
Collection of the Wyeth Foundation for American Art

Andrew Wyeth
Untitled (#2320), 1936
Charcoal on paper
23.88" x 18.75"
Collection of the Wyeth Foundation for American Art

Wyeth Exhibition Checklist *(continued)*

Andrew Wyeth
Undercover Study, 1970
Pencil on paper
18" x 23.63"
Collection of the Wyeth Foundation for American Art

Andrew Wyeth
Undercover Study, 1970
Watercolor on paper´
21.63" x 28.75"
Collection of the Wyeth Foundation for American Art

Andrew Wyeth
Untitled (#2297), 1938
Pencil on paper
16 1/2" x 22"
Collection of the Wyeth Foundation for American Art

Andrew Wyeth
The Clearing Study, 1979
Pencil on paper
28.38" x 14"
Collection of the Wyeth Foundation for American Art

Andrew Wyeth
The Clearing Study, 1979
Pencil on paper
16 3/4" x 14"
Collection of the Wyeth Foundation for American Art

Andrew Wyeth
The Clearing Study, 1979
Watercolor and pencil on paper
32 3/4" x 21 3/4"
Collection of the Wyeth Foundation for American Art

Andrew Wyeth
Scuba Study, 1994
Pencil on paper
18" x 24"
Collection of the Wyeth Foundation for American Art

Andrew Wyeth
Day Dream Study, 1980
Drybrush and pencil on paper
21 3/4" x 39 3/4"
Collection of the Wyeth Foundation for American Art

Plaster model after Houdon's Study for *Saint John the Baptist*,
n.d. 29" H
Collection of the Wyeth Foundation for American Art

JAMIE WYETH (American, b. 1946)

Jamie Wyeth
Sketchbook with Studies of Rudolf Nureyev, 1977
Pen and ink on paper
14" x 11"
Brandywine River Museum of Art, Purchased with funds from the
Robert J. Kleberg Jr. and Helen C. Kleberg Foundation; Roemer
Foundation; the Margaret Dorrance Strawbridge Foundation of
PAI, Inc.; and an anonymous donor, 2006

Jamie Wyeth
Black Wash Background, Torso, Nureyev (Study #14), 1977
Mixed media, pencil, and wash on paper
16 1/2" x 20 1/2"
Brandywine River Museum of Art, Purchased with funds given in
memory of Dr. Margaret I. Handy, 1980

Jamie Wyeth
Unfinished Coat, in Fur, Nureyev (Study #13), 1977
Pencil and wash on paper
20 1/2" x 16 1/2"
Brandywine River Museum of Art, Purchased with funds given in
memory of Dr. Margaret I. Handy, 1980

Jamie Wyeth
Nureyev as the Faune, 1977/2002
Combined mediums on toned board
20" x 16"
Brandywine River Museum of Art, Purchased with funds from the
Robert J. Kleberg Jr. and Helen C. Kleberg Foundation; Roemer
Foundation; the Margaret Dorrance Strawbridge Foundation of
PAI, Inc.; and an anonymous donor, 2006

Jamie Wyeth
Sketchbook Image, N-31a, 1977
Pen and ink
11" x 14"
Brandywine River Museum of Art, Purchased with funds from
the Robert J. Kleberg, Jr. and Helen C. Kleberg Foundation;
the Roemer Foundation; the Margaret Dorrance Strawbridge
Foundation of PAI, Inc.; and an anonymous donor, 2006

Jamie Wyeth
Morgue Drawing Deltoid, 1965
Pencil on paper, anatomical sketchbook, page 1, recto
14" x 11"
The Phyllis and Jamie Wyeth Collection

Jamie Wyeth
Morgue Drawing Two Hands, 1965
Pencil on paper, anatomical sketchbook, page 3
11" x 14"
The Phyllis and Jamie Wyeth Collection

Jamie Wyeth
Morgue Drawing Five Hands, 1965
Pencil on paper, anatomical sketchbook, page 4
11" x 14"
The Phyllis and Jamie Wyeth Collection

Jamie Wyeth
Morgue Drawing Three Hands, 1965
Pencil on paper, anatomical sketchbook, page 5
11" x 14"
The Phyllis and Jamie Wyeth Collection

Jamie Wyeth
Morgue Drawing Clavicle, 1965
Pencil on paper, anatomical sketchbook, page 6
14" x 11"
The Phyllis and Jamie Wyeth Collection

Jamie Wyeth
Morgue Drawing Neck,1965
Pencil on paper, anatomical sketchbook, page 7
11" x 14"
The Phyllis and Jamie Wyeth Collection

Jamie Wyeth
Morgue Drawing Skull, 1965
Pencil on paper, anatomical sketchbook, page 8, recto
11" x 14"
The Phyllis and Jamie Wyeth Collection

Jamie Wyeth
Morgue Drawing Three Skulls One Head, 1965
Pencil on paper, anatomical sketchbook, page 9
11" x 14"
The Phyllis and Jamie Wyeth Collection

Jamie Wyeth
Orca Bates (Study #1), 1990
Charcoal and conte crayon on brown cardboard
40" x 37 1/4"
The Phyllis and Jamie Wyeth Collection

Jamie Wyeth
Red Nureyev—The Phyllis M. Wyeth "Nureyev Suite," 1977/2020
Charcoal, wash, gesso, and watercolor on Twin Rocker Handmade Paper
41" x 34"
The Phyllis and Jamie Wyeth Collection

Jamie Wyeth
Pig Drawing, 1969
Pencil on paper
10" x 13"
The Phyllis and Jamie Wyeth Collection

Jamie Wyeth
Pig Drawing, Head, 1969
Pencil on paper
14 1/4" x 15 3/4"
The Phyllis and Jamie Wyeth Collection

Jamie Wyeth
Study of a Pig Lying Down, 1969
Pencil on paper
13 1/2" x 11"
The Phyllis and Jamie Wyeth Collection

Jamie Wyeth
Pig Drawing, Head, 1969
Pencil on paper
14 1/4" x 16 3/4"
The Phyllis and Jamie Wyeth Collection

Jamie Wyeth
Pig Drawing, Reclining, 1969
Pencil on paper
10" x 13 1/4"
The Phyllis and Jamie Wyeth Collection

Jamie Wyeth
Pig Drawing, Two Heads, 1969
Pencil on paper
14" x 11 1/8"
The Phyllis and Jamie Wyeth Collection

Jamie Wyeth
Morgue Drawing, Cadaver, 1965
Graphite on paper
11" x 14"
Collection of the Wyeth Foundation for American Art

Lenders to the Exhibitions

Museums / Institutions
Brandywine River Museum of Art
Colquitt County Arts Center
La Salle University Art Museum
The Phyllis and Jamie Wyeth Collection
Portland Museum of Art
The Wyeth Foundation for American Art

Private Collections
Debra Campbell
Thomas Carpenter Keiper
Dan Ostermiller

Assistance with Exhibition Development

Jamie Wyeth
Nicky Wyeth
Judy Kopff

Image Permissions

All Andrew Wyeth images © 2022 Andrew Wyeth/
    Artists Rights Society (ARS)
All Jamie Wyeth images © 2022 Jamie Wyeth/
    Artists Rights Society (ARS)

N.C. Wyeth Artwork
Brandywine River Museum
Colquitt County Arts Center
Thomas Keiper
LaSalle University Art Museum
Dan Ostermiller
Portland Museum of Art
The Wyeth Foundation for American Art

Carolyn Wyeth Artwork
Brandywine River Museum of Art

Andrew Wyeth Artwork
The Wyeth Foundation for American Art

Jamie Wyeth Artwork
Brandywine River Museum of Art
The Phyllis and Jamie Wyeth Collection
The Wyeth Foundation for American Art